# The Surpris

"Shhh! We are going to a surprise party."

2

"You can come, too."

3

"Shhh! We are going to a surprise party."

"You can come, too."

"Shhh! We are going to a surprise party."

"You can come, too."

"Shhh! We are going to a surprise party."

"You can come, too."

"Shhh! We are going to a surprise party."

"You can come, too."

"Shhh! We are going to a surprise party."

"You can come, too."

13

"Shhh! We are going to a surprise party."

16